728

As you read this book you will be able to find th[e] questions about yourself and the way you do t[...] is based on part of the popular 'Living and Working [...] exhibition at **EUREKA! The Museum for Children** in Halifax. **EUREKA!** is the first museum in Great Britain designed especially for children. The Museum's exhibitions use an exciting new approach, placing the child at the centre of learning, and the book has been designed to bring the best of the exhibition into your home or classroom.

The book is full of activities and information. It offers plenty of talking points for children and adults and shows how learning together can be fun. The book will appeal to the child in us all.

EUREKA! The Museum for Children 1994

> I want to know all about what goes on inside a house. Will you help me to find out?

ACKNOWLEDGEMENTS

Random House Children's Books would like to thank the following
for their kind co-operation in the making of this book:
The staff of Bounds Green Junior School and Kenmont Primary School,
Sally Charlton and all the children who appear in the photographs.
Models from EUREKA! and exhibition design by
Tim Hunkin, Satoshi Kitamura and Greville White

Photography by Katie Vandyck and Peter Millard
Design by Mandy Sherliker

First published 1994

1 3 5 7 9 10 8 6 4 2

Text © Stephen Webster 1994
Illustrations © Satoshi Kitamura 1994
Stephen Webster and Satoshi Kitamura have asserted their
right under the Copyright, Designs and Patents Act, 1988
to be identified as the author and illustrator of this work.

First published in the United Kingdom in 1994 by
Riverswift
Random House, 20 Vauxhall Bridge Road, London SW1V 2SA

Random House Australia (Pty) Limited
20 Alfred Street, Milsons Point, Sydney,
New South Wales 2061, Australia

Random House New Zealand Limited
18 Poland Road, Glenfield
Auckland 10, New Zealand

Random House South Africa (Pty) Limited
PO Box 337, Bergvlei, South Africa

Random House UK Limited Reg. No. 954009

The EUREKA! series of books is based on the displays at
EUREKA! The Museum for Children, Discovery Road, Halifax,
Yorkshire, England, HX1 2NE. Tel: 0422 330069

A CIP Catalogue record for this book is
available from the British Library

ISBN 1 898304 31 9
Printed in Hong Kong

Inside My House

A **EUREKA!**™ Book

Stephen Webster

Illustrations by Satoshi Kitamura

RIVERSWIFT

LONDON

My Home

Hello, I'm Tweet. As I sit here in my nest, I get a good view of you all in your homes. My home is simple but yours look very interesting. Will you tell me about the way you live?

Thousands and thousands of years ago someone in your family probably lived in a cave or a shelter made from branches. Your ancestors needed homes where they were safe from wild animals and the worst of the weather. A home was a place to come back to after a day of searching for food. When the fires were lit, home was a place of warmth and shelter. Nothing's changed much has it? You still want your home to be safe and warm and dry.

For some people home is a tent or a caravan. For others it is a flat, a bungalow or a house.

What's yours? What do you miss most when you're away? The food? Your own things? The bathroom? Your family?

Tweet investigates

Note it down
Think about your own home. Write down the things that make it special for you.

Experiment
Make a den for yourself under the table, behind the sofa or inside a big cardboard box. Live in it for an hour or two. What will you need?

I suppose people and animals need homes for the same reasons - shelter and warmth and a safe place to sleep, eat and raise our children.

Who lives here?

There isn't much room in my nest, especially as the baby birds grow so fast. Who do you share your home with, and how do you manage to get along?

Most children live with at least one grown-up, sometimes other children, and quite often some animals too. So most of you probably share your home with quite a few other people. And there is usually one particular room where you all get together – maybe the kitchen or the living room.

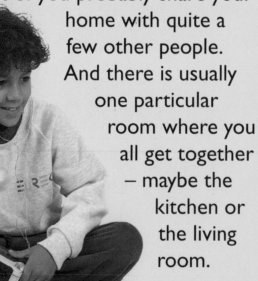

It's not always easy sharing a room, is it? What happens when one person wants to listen to music and another wants to read quietly? Or when you all want to watch something different on TV? Or what if the youngest child wants to stay up later than the oldest one?

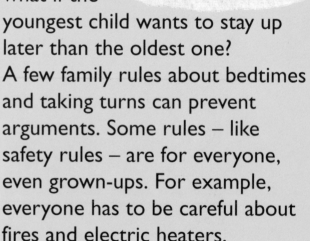

A few family rules about bedtimes and taking turns can prevent arguments. Some rules – like safety rules – are for everyone, even grown-ups. For example, everyone has to be careful about fires and electric heaters.

Tweet investigates

Note it down
Make a list of all the members of your household, including pets. Write down your close neighbours too if you live in a flat.

Talk
Talk about the rules in your house and how they are decided. Are they fair? What rules do you think are important?

You all need a few rules to help things run smoothly. Are there any other places in your house where you have to take extra care?

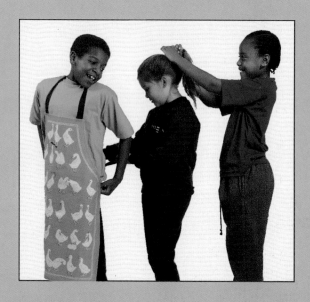

The Kitchen

> My chicks don't mind a bit of earth with their worms, but it seems that you need to follow a few hygiene rules when you prepare food in your kitchens.

The kitchen is where you prepare and cook your food. You wash the dishes there and probably do the laundry as well.

It is important that the place where food is prepared and stored is kept clean and free from germs.

You can keep food fresh by putting it in the fridge. It's cold enough in there to slow down the growth of germs.

A freezer is even colder so food can be stored for longer.

If you're working with food you must be clean too.

If you've got long hair tie it back, and always wash your hands. Now you're ready for your favourite recipe. Don't forget to clear up afterwards and wipe the surfaces clean again.

Tweet investigates

Experiment

Here is a scientific experiment that tastes good! First make sure you have a grown-up nearby. Toast a piece of bread. Note down how the bread changes. Is it soft or crisp? Cold or hot? Does it change colour? Now butter the toast and note down what happens to the butter (or margarine!). Does it turn into liquid? Cut the toast and see how far the butter has sunk into the bread. Now you can eat your experiment.

Talk

There are lots of things to sort in a kitchen. Fruit and vegetables go in different places, so where will you put the tomatoes? Which foods should always go in the fridge?

A special place for preparing food seems like a good idea to me. Do you have any other special rooms?

The Bathroom

I wash in the local puddle. But you have a special room for washing with hot and cold water on tap. How does the water get there?

You use lots of water every day for washing and for flushing the toilet. You even like splashing about and playing with water. It's easy to forget how precious it is. If you feel like having a shower or bath, you can just go to the bathroom, turn on the taps and wash. So how does water get into the taps? Sometimes you can see some big water pipes when the road is being dug up. They are carrying supplies from a reservoir, a lake where water is stored. Smaller pipes run beneath the pavement into each home or block of flats. Once inside your home the water flows along the pipes to the taps or a tank. Taps are at the end of pipes, and block the water until you open them.

When you flush the toilet, water rushes out from toilet and pushes your waste round the S-bend. The large pipe just beneath the toilet drains away the waste, out of the house and down into the sewers.

Tweet investigates

Experiment

Think about the way water moves. Does it flow up or down? Now try some ways of moving water from one place to another (either outside or in the bath). Can you find out how a siphon or a toy pump works?

Write

Imagine what it would be like if there was no running water and write a description of your day.

At EUREKA! Archimedes is lowered into his bath. The water overflows and runs down. It is brought up again by the 'Archimedes screw' that carries the water up as it turns.

Personally I think it sounds easier to go to the water than to bring the water to you ...

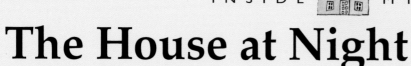

The House at Night

Before I sleep I make sure my chicks are warm and safe. Then I put my head under my wing and nod off. What is night-time like in your home?

Everybody needs to feel warm and safe before they go to sleep, and so does the house. The grown-ups lock the doors, draw the curtains and switch everything off. How do you prepare for sleep? Probably first of all you change into your nightclothes, brush your teeth and say goodnight. Do you have a bedtime story, a favourite toy or a night light? Are there things you like to think about, just before you go to sleep?

Lights make us forget the dark outside. How do you feel when the lights go out and everything looks different?

At night other animals are quite active. Minibeasts crawl out of their hiding places and search for food. Cats like to hunt and explore but a dog is happier to sleep and dream.

Tweet investigates

Note it down
Write or draw some of the things which help to make you ready for sleep.

Draw
Make a night-time picture of the shapes and shadows you see when the lights are turned off.

Make
How would you change your room? Cut out pictures from magazines to design a bedroom.

I like the peace and quiet of night-time too. There are fewer cars and all you people stay in one place.

Comings and Goings

Your homes seem to have a life of their own. Sometimes they are quiet, sometimes they are busy. What's going on?

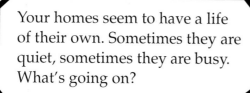

Have you ever thought about all the comings and goings in your home? Every morning you go out to school. Every afternoon you come back again. The letters come through the letterbox. Shopping is brought in, rubbish is put out. Clean water comes in pipes. Dirty water goes down the drains. Electric cables bring electricity. Telephone wires carry messages. TV and radio signals are beamed in. Your home is a busy place. Even the pets come and go.

What would your home be like if none of this happened?

Tweet investigates

Write

Pretend you are a spider in the corner and describe a day in your life in the house.

Experiment

Find out where your electricity and gas meters are. Why do the numbers go round?

Draw

Make a time chart, showing how your home is busy or quiet at different times of the day.

> It must be strange to have so many things coming into your house when you can't even see them!

High Days and Holidays

Sometimes I see lots of people arriving at your house, and they stay for a long time. I want to find out more about these get-togethers.

Families and friends gather together in each other's homes to celebrate an anniversary like a golden wedding, or a festival like Chinese New Year. You often dress up for family celebrations and usually you share a special meal. It might just be your favourite food or it might be a meal that you eat in memory of something that happened long ago. Jews eat a flat bread with their Passover meal because when their ancestors

were escaping from Egypt 3,000 years ago there wasn't time to wait for the bread to rise. Sweets are part of a lot of celebrations. So are candles and fireworks, singing and dancing, and of course, best of all, presents!

Tweet investigates

Make
Make a calendar showing the birthdays and festivals in your home.

Talk
Find out from someone of another religion the names of their feast days. What is their favourite food?

> I can see that life in your home is often a lot of fun. But what about the housework?

In the Hindu summer celebration of Raksha Bandham a sister ties red and gold threads around her brother's wrist to protect him. He gives her a present in return.

House Work

I'm always trying to get my nest tidy. I see that you have a lot of work to do as well. How does the work get divided up?

If nobody ever cleared up or washed anything your home would soon be very messy and dirty. So who does the housework in your family? Do you do your share? Washing up, tidying, cleaning, hoovering and doing the laundry are all household chores. They can be boring jobs, so it's best if they are shared round the family. Modern machines like the vacuum cleaner and the washing machine make housework much easier. Your grandparents will probably remember when each job took a whole day. Monday was spent doing the washing, Tuesday the ironing. Friday was usually baking day. Having your own special jobs to do can be fun.

It's nice to sit down and relax when you have helped to make everything clean and tidy.

Tweet investigates

Note it down
Make a rota dividing up the housework fairly.

Draw
Draw or make a house robot. How will it make life easier?

Write
Write a poem describing one of the household tasks you do each week.

I'm glad you do some of the housework. I wish my chicks were as good ...

Eco-Homes

> I'm glad to say that everything in my nest is completely recycled and eco-friendly. Can the same be said about your home?

Many of the things that make our lives comfortable are not so good for all the other living things on this planet. Power stations that produce electricity, factories that make the things we use every day and cars and lorries all give off dirty fumes and gases. Even farmers and gardeners kill pests with poisons that can harm other wildlife. But if every single person, including you, tries to be less wasteful, the world can become a safer place for all wildlife. Here are some things you can do to help:

• Save electricity by switching off the TV and lights when you go out of a room.

• Sort your rubbish so that bottles, cans and papers can go to be recycled.

• Don't run the tap when you clean your teeth.

• Make sure that you never drop sweetpapers or drink cans in the street.

•Find out more about the wildlife that lives around your home – there's plenty of it!

A house is a good refuge for spiders which do a useful job catching and eating the flies and insects that come inside. Birds find shelter on window ledges, gutters and roof tops. Try putting bird seeds and old crusts of bread on a windowsill during the hard winter months. Choose a quiet place, safely away from cats, and you'll be visited by hungry blackbirds, robins and tits.

Tweet investigates

Note it down
Could your house save energy? Make a list. Are lights left on? Are the windows draughty? Is the loft insulated?

Make
Recycle some of your junk into a junk model.

Draw
Draw the minibeasts that live in and around your house.

I'm glad you care about the environment - that means you care about me!

Looking after the House

I'm always repairing my nest, replacing twigs and securing it in the tree. Do you have repairs too?

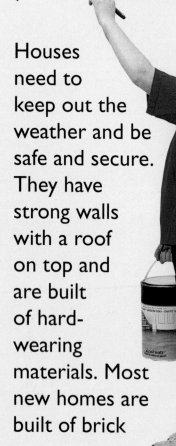

Houses need to keep out the weather and be safe and secure. They have strong walls with a roof on top and are built of hard-wearing materials. Most new homes are built of brick or concrete. Probably you'll never see the most important part of your house. Buried beneath you are the foundations, the part of the walls built under-ground. The foundations hold up the walls.

When you go outside your house, look up at the roof. Can you see the gutters running along the top of the walls? They collect the rain, and make sure it flows down drainpipes, away from the walls. It's important to keep the rain out of a house. That's why people have to make sure the roof is in good repair, the gutters aren't blocked by leaves, and all the woodwork is protected by paint.

Tweet investigates

Experiment

Build a structure from straws or Lego. Test it for strength by blowing it and by resting weights on top. What makes a strong shape?

Write

Write down your own version of The Three Little Pigs story, ready for someone younger than you. Make a tape of the story, or a board book.

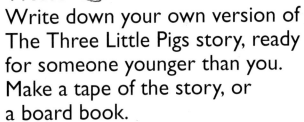

I can see now that your homes only stay up if they are looked after. Then they can last for a very long time.

History in the House

> I like to repair my old nest or build a new one every year. I wouldn't dream of moving into someone else's. But you almost certainly live in a home others have lived in before you.

Some old houses feel warm and welcoming – others feel spooky and threatening. Perhaps it has something to do with all the people who lived there.

Most people live in houses that are at least five years old. Some houses are hundreds of years old. Imagine all the comings and goings those old houses must have seen!

You can usually find some clues to the history of your home if you look. You might find old wallpaper inside a wardrobe or yellowing newspapers under the carpet. Better still, there might be old letters and photographs in the attic that tell you about the previous owners.

Old houses are mysterious sometimes. There is always a place where old machines and broken toys get slowly forgotten, and stay, waiting to be discovered again. For some homes this hiding place is the attic. For others it is a big cupboard or even a space under the bed. Wherever it is in your home, you'll probably find some surprises there.

Tweet investigates

Talk

Ask in your local library if there is a book with photographs of your area. See if you can find your street. Talk to one of the older residents in your street about the changes they have seen.

Write

If a house could talk, what would it say? Write a story or make a picture showing some of the adventures of a haunted house.

> I wonder what you will leave behind in your house for the next people to find?

Moving House

I fly off to my winter quarters every year, so I'm used to moving around. It's not as if I have anything to take with me! But you all seem to have so much stuff. What happens if you want to move?

Sometimes you have to move house. Perhaps it's because there is a new baby and your family wants more space. Or maybe one of the grown-ups has another job. Before you go all the furniture has to be packed up and the plates and pans and books and toys have to be put in boxes. A big removal van arrives to carry all your things off to the new home.

It's exciting to move somewhere new and maybe have more space or a bigger garden. A lot of things stay the same. Your family is still there, and your pets and your possessions. Even if you go to a new school and make new friends, you know that home hasn't changed much.

Going on holiday is a kind of move too. You have to decide what you need, get packed up, and do some travelling. For a short while you have a new home, camping, staying with relatives or living in a hotel. It's good to learn about living in different places and still know that soon you will be safely home.

Well, I've really learned a lot about you and your families and what goes on in your homes. But I'll still be watching you from my nest. Goodbye!

Tweet investigates

Draw

Make a cartoon story about the adventures of a cat when the family moves house.

Write

Pretend you are going on holiday. Make a list of all the things you'll want to pack.

INDEX